Darling

Valentine's Day Coloring Book

Color Your Heart, Color your Love

Kimberly Harold

Happy Coloring

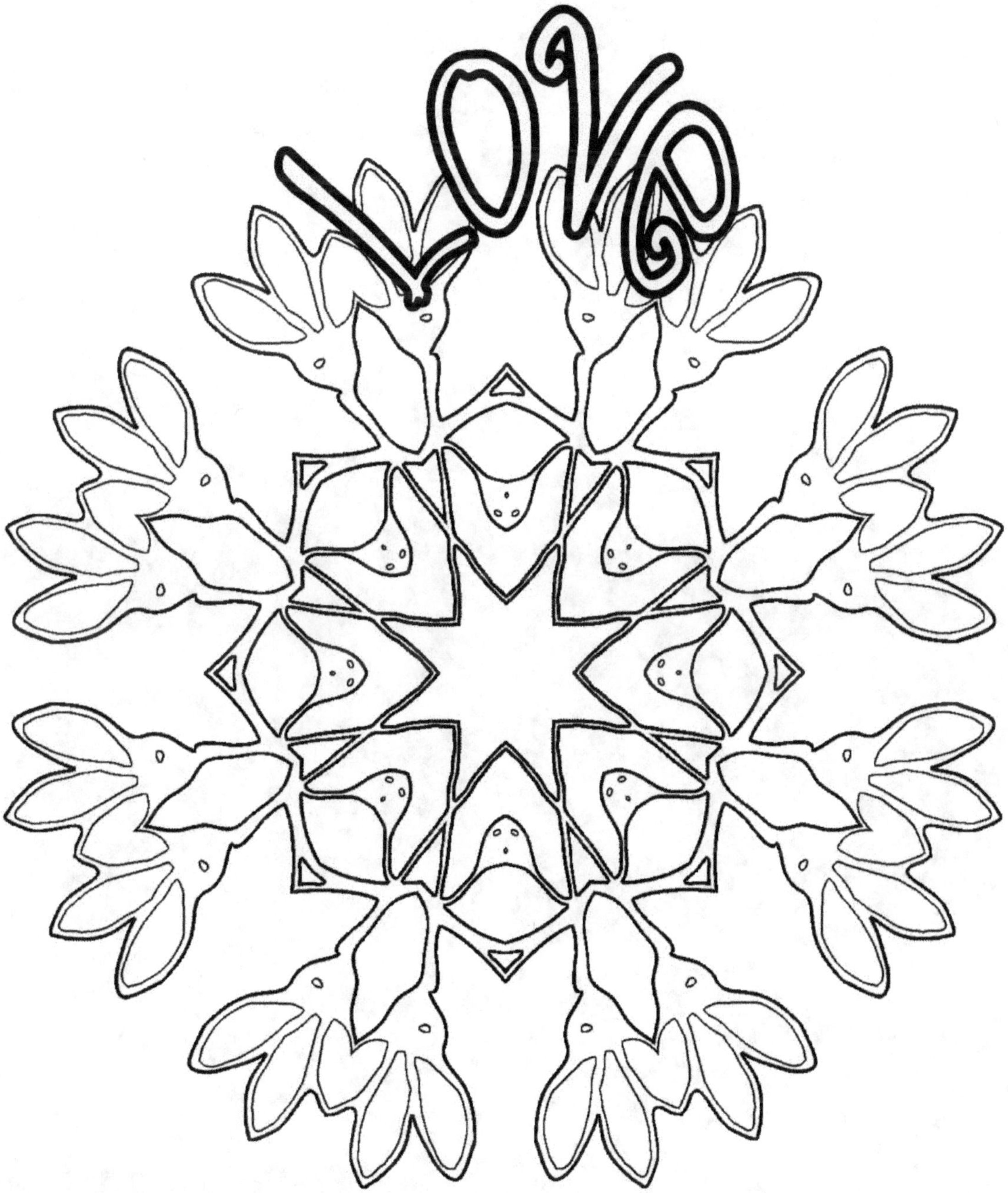
Love

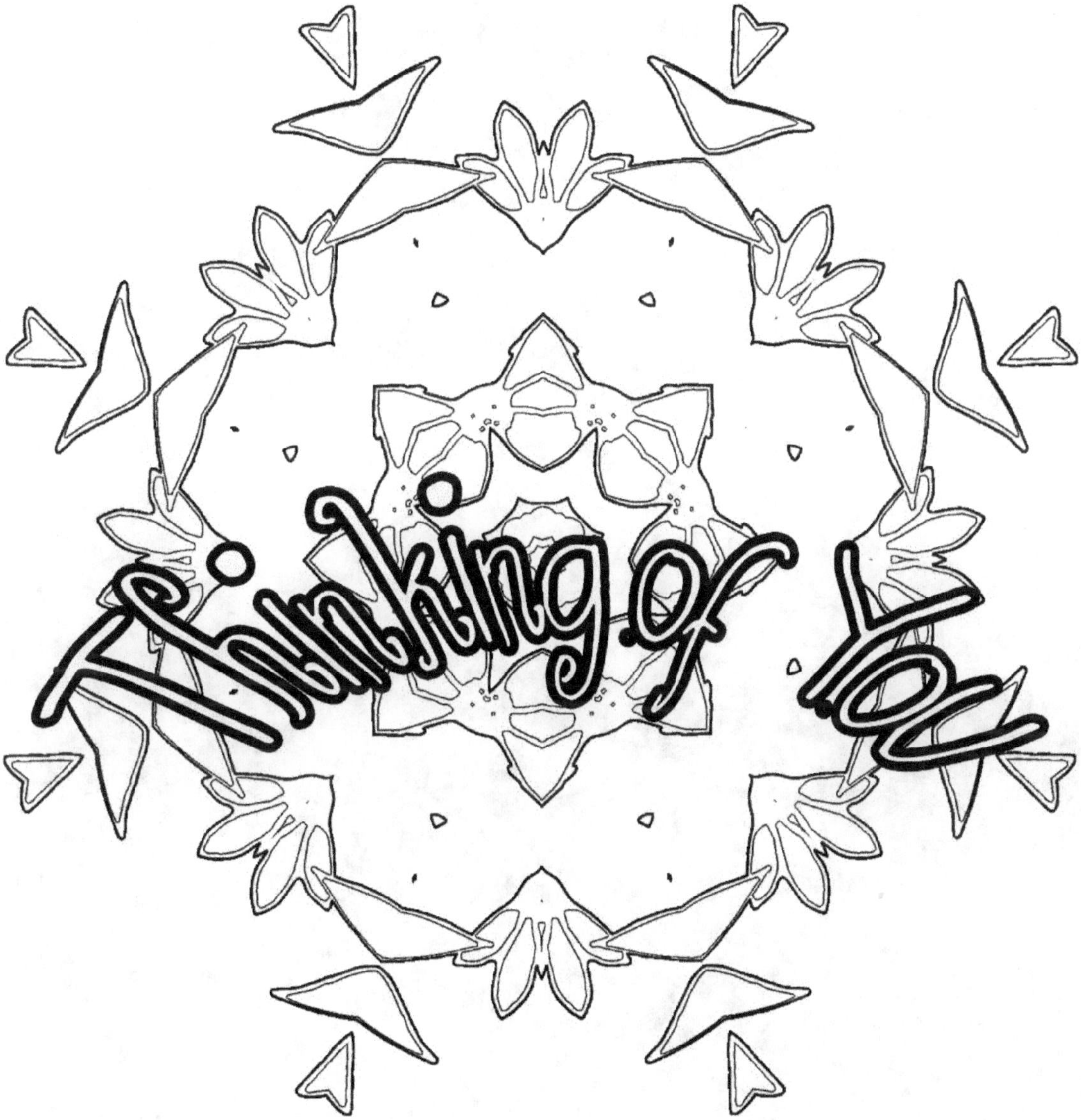
Thinking of You

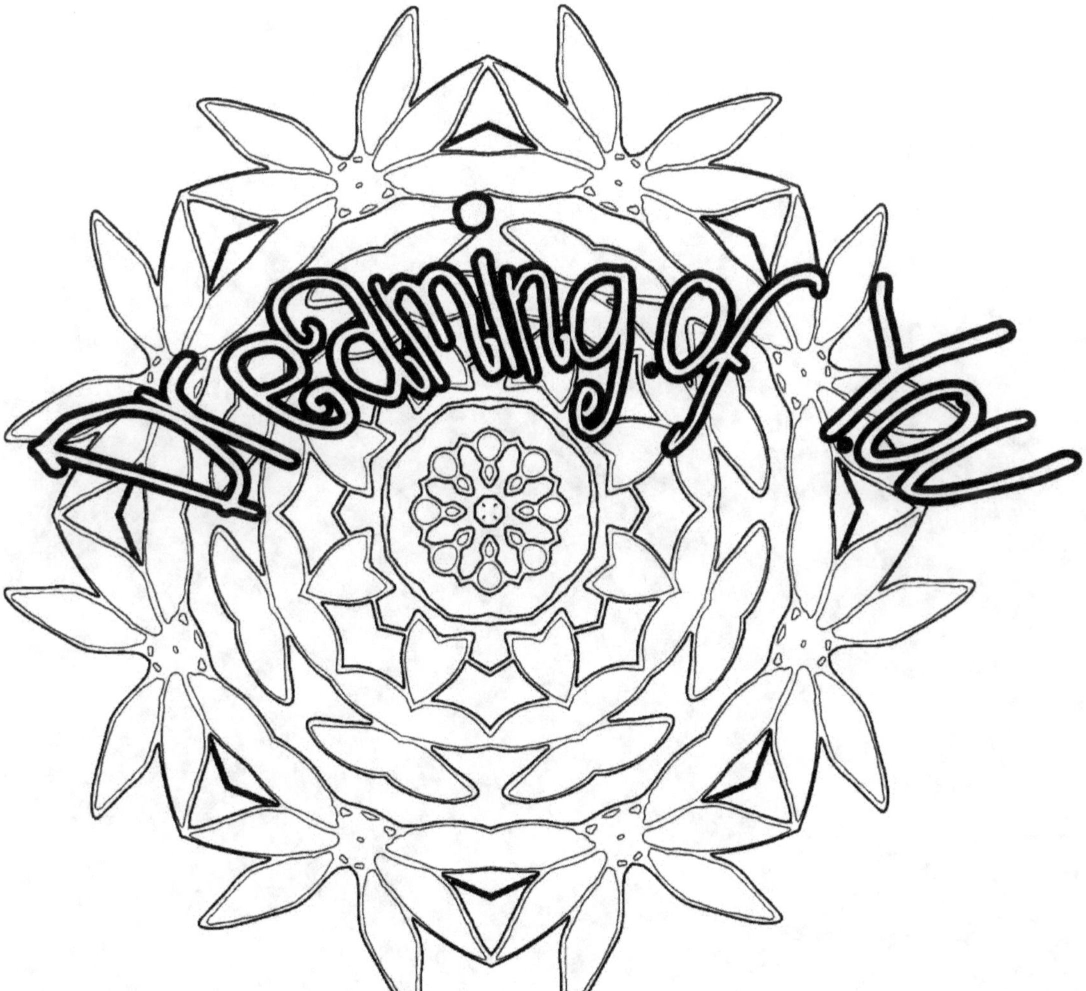
Dreaming of You

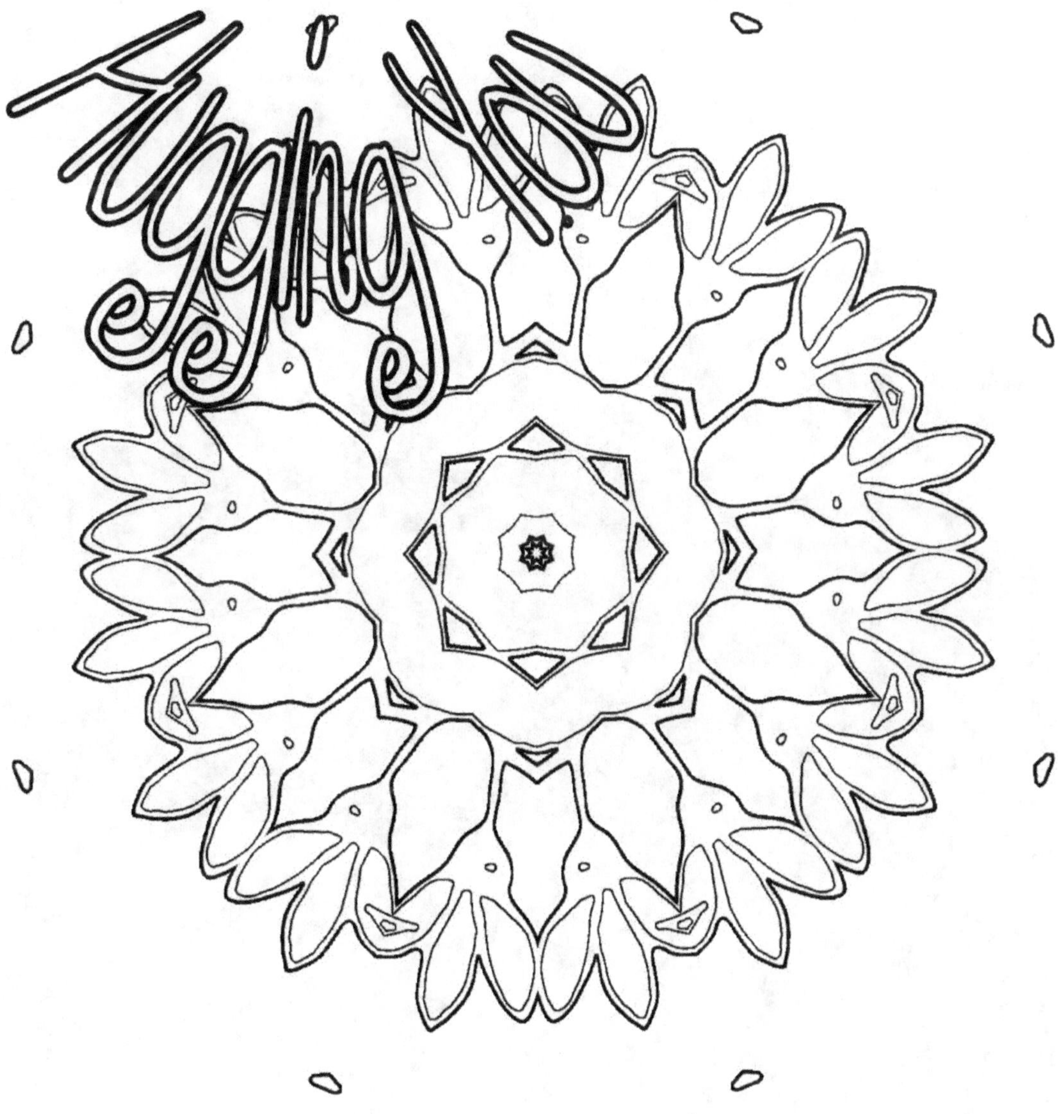
Hugging You

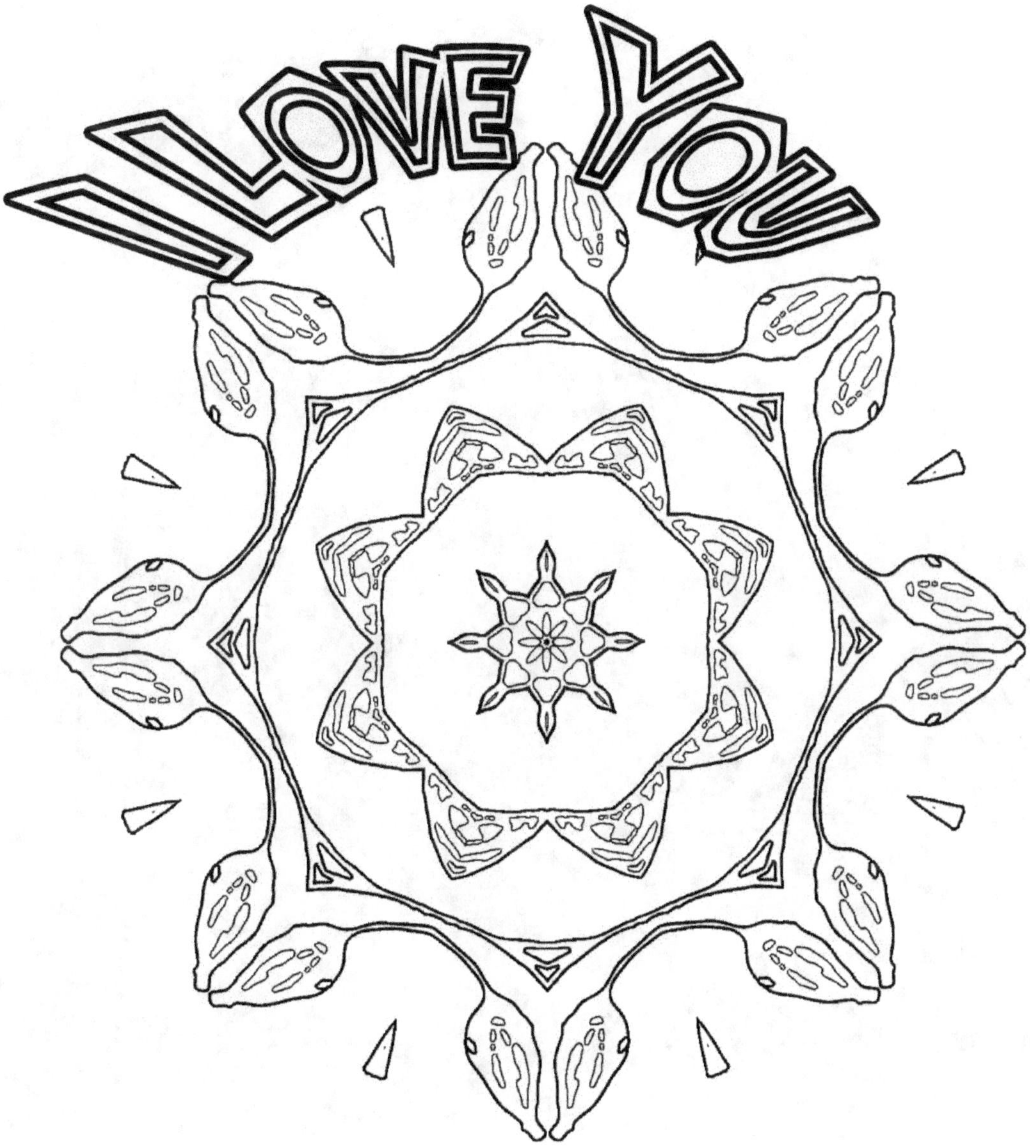
I LOVE YOU

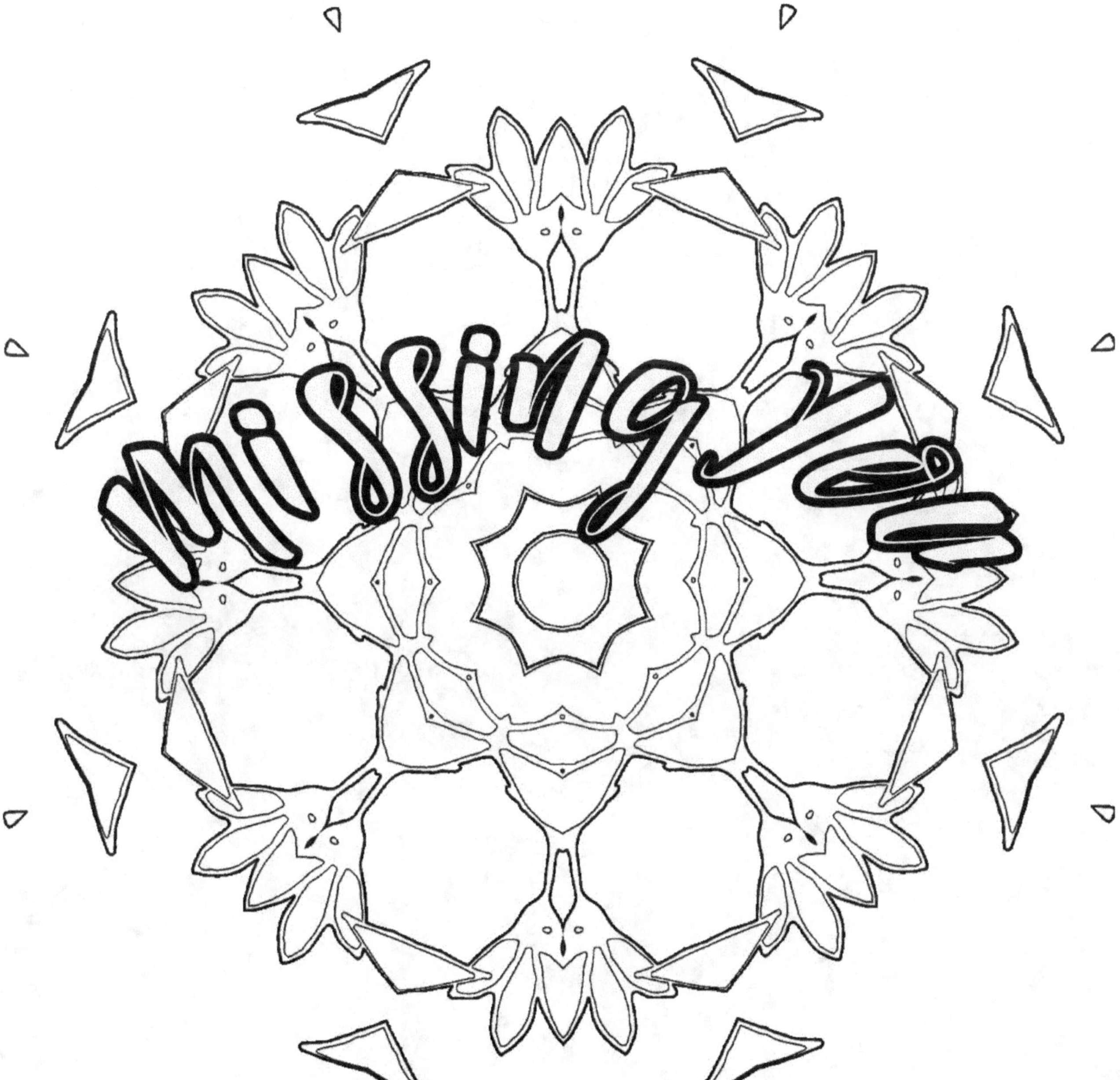
missing you

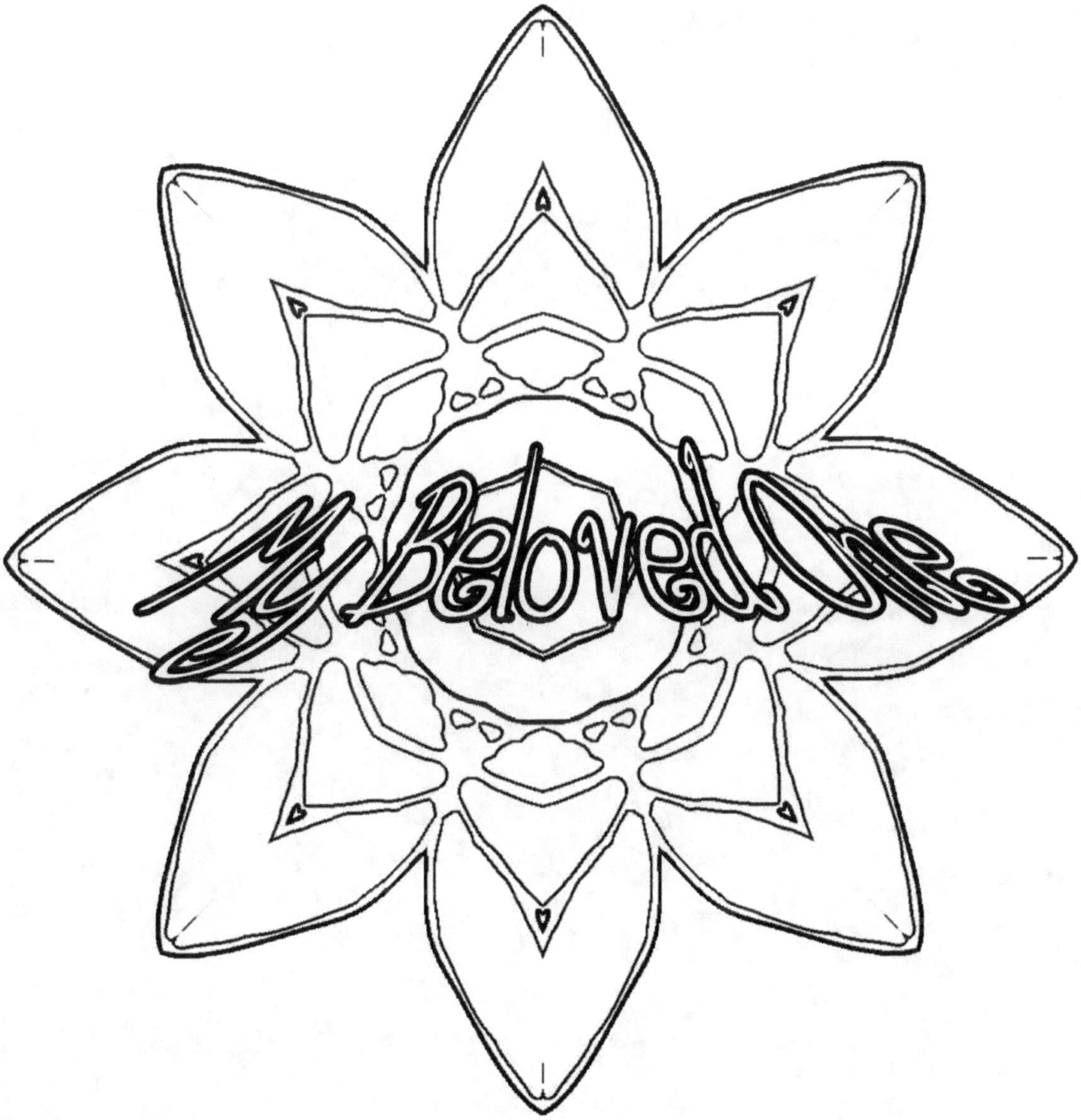
My Beloved One

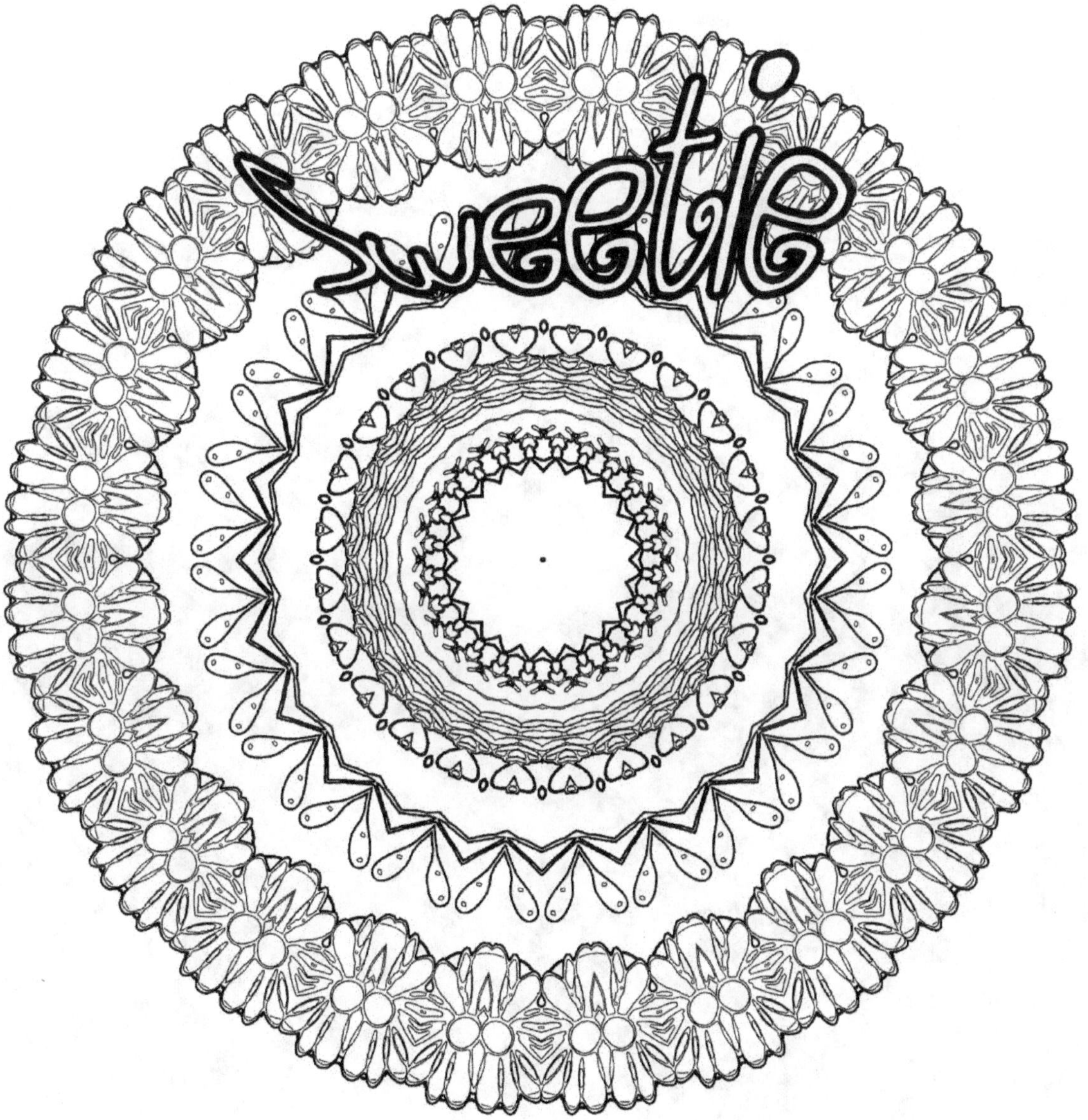
Sweetie

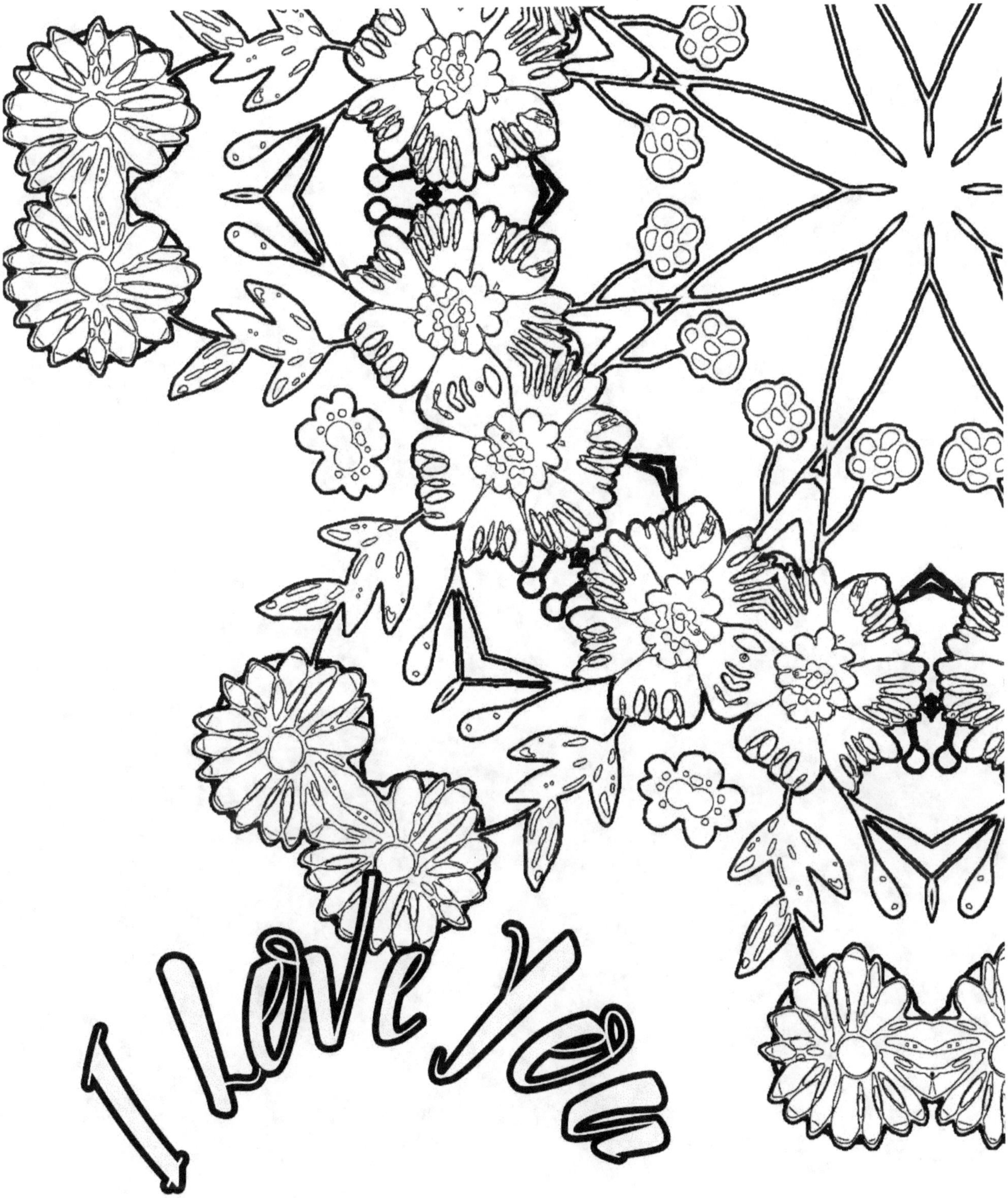
I Love You

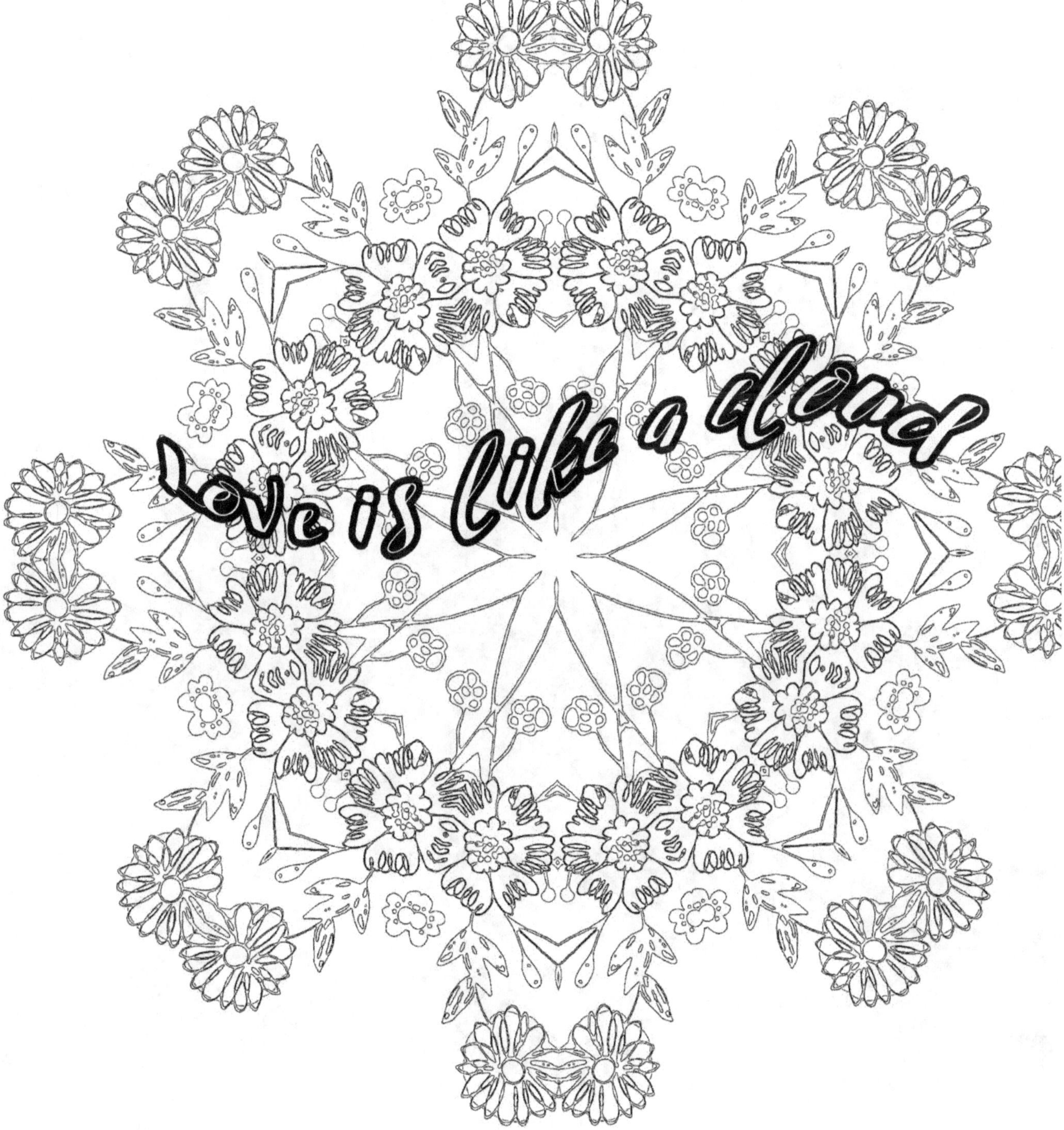
Love is like a cloud

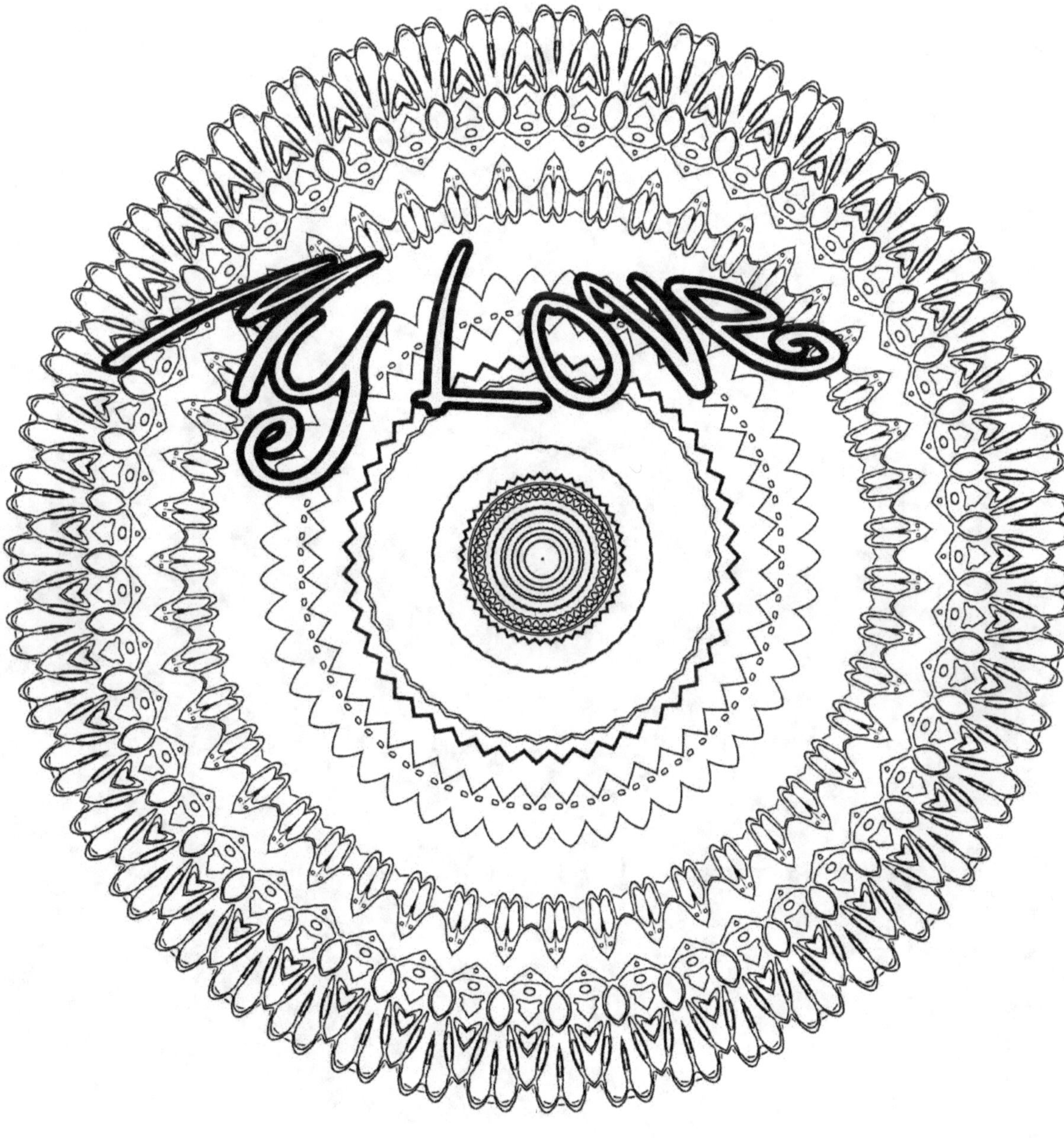
My Love

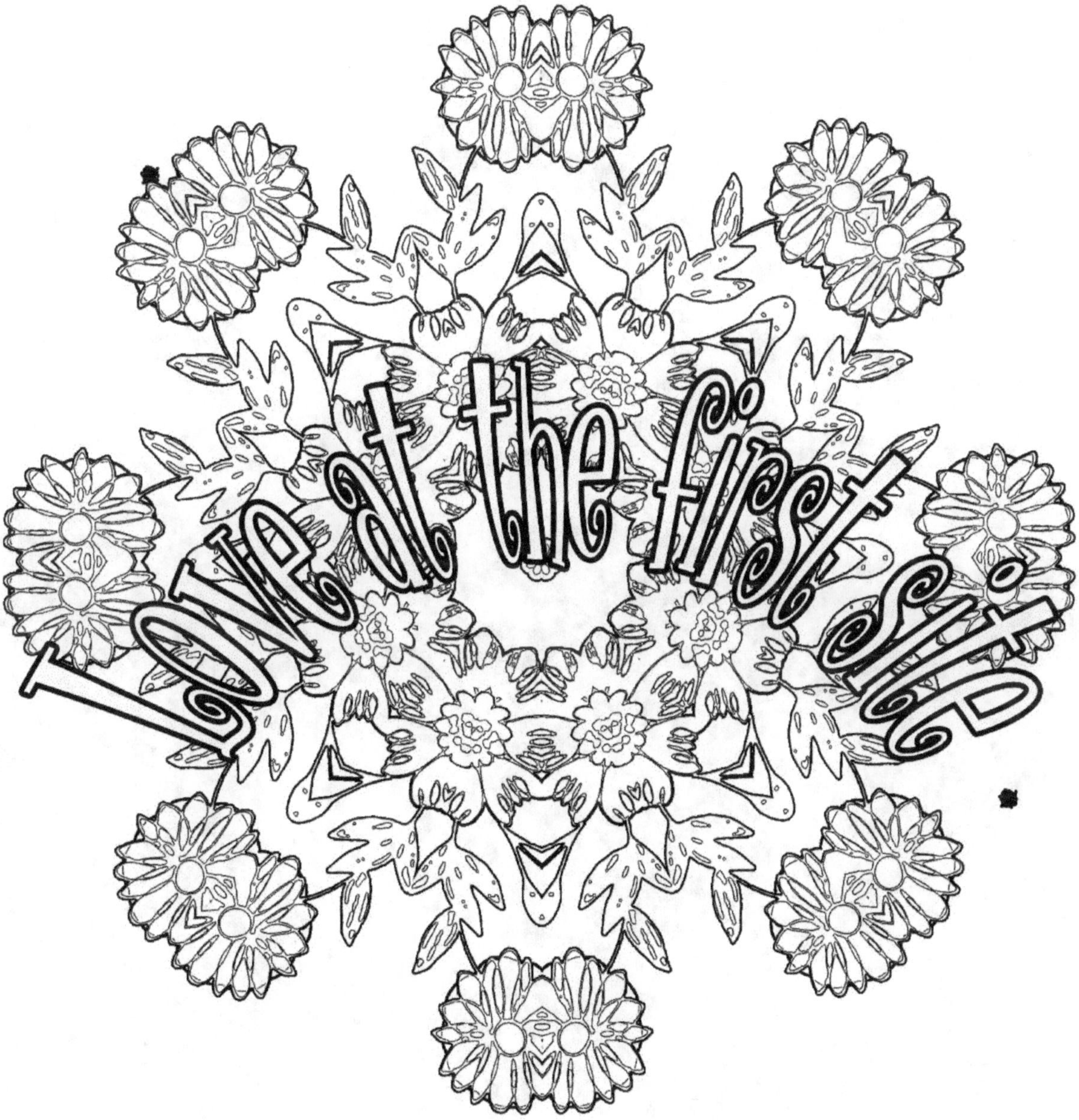
Love at the first site

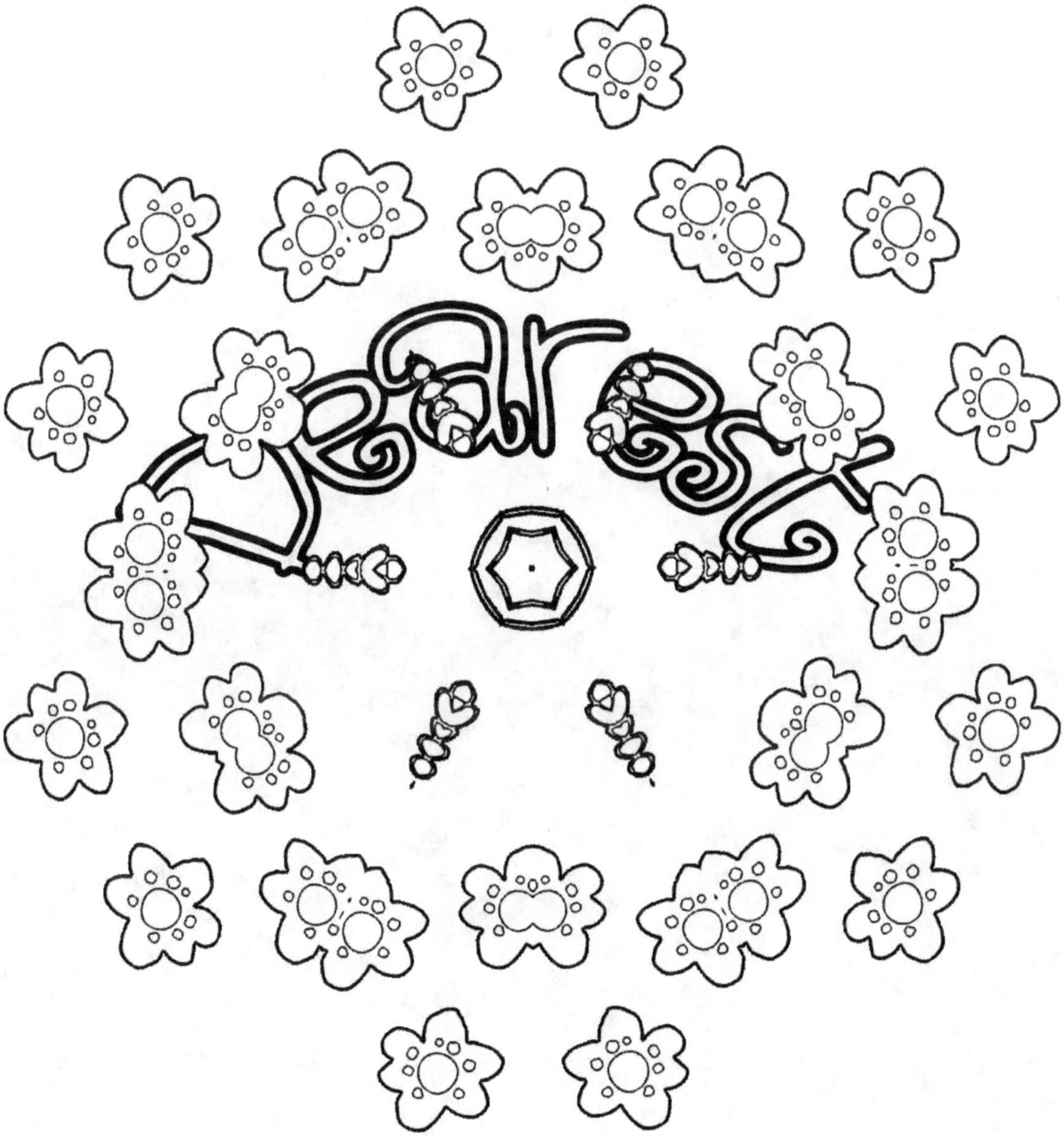
Dearest

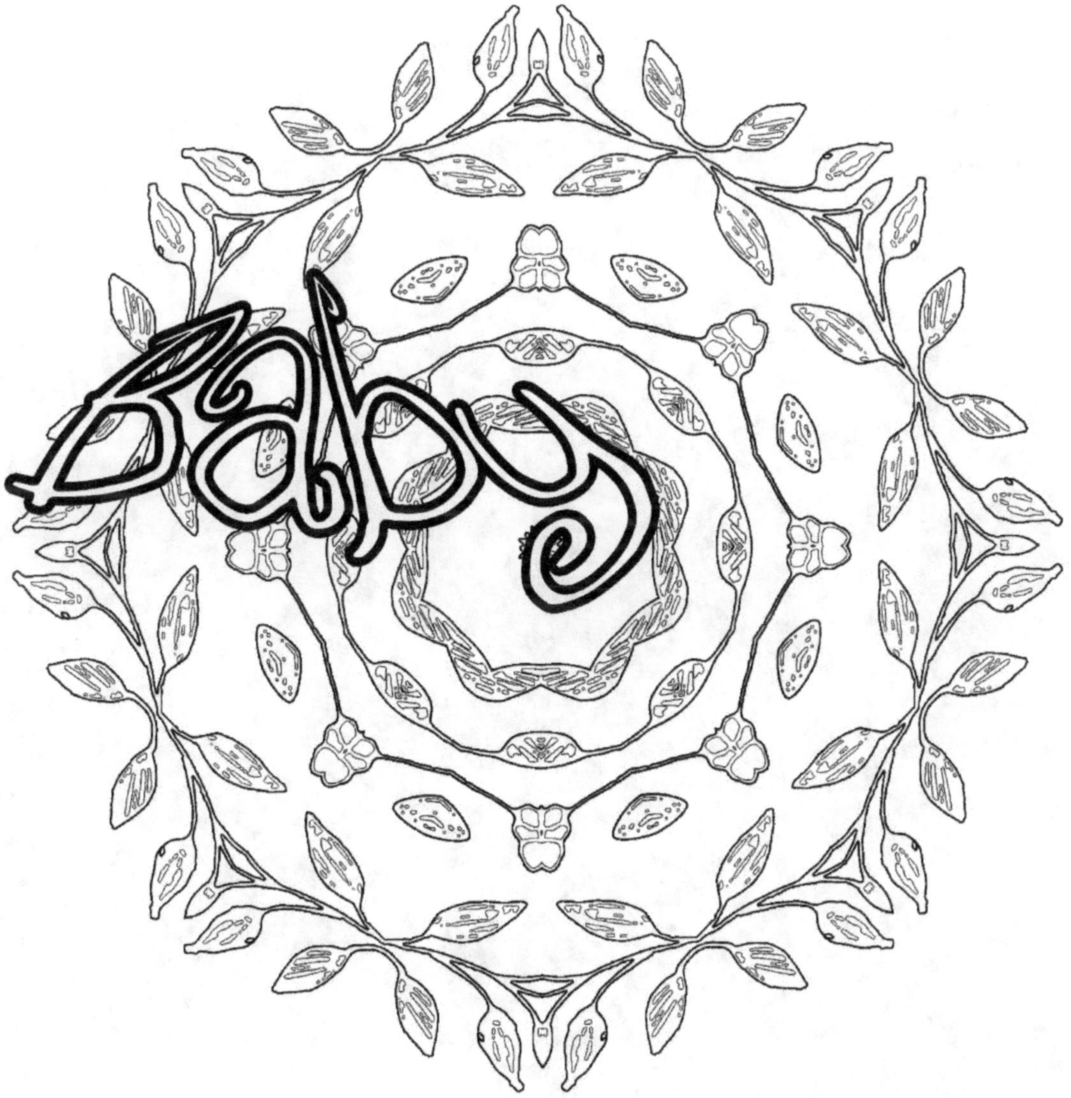
Baby

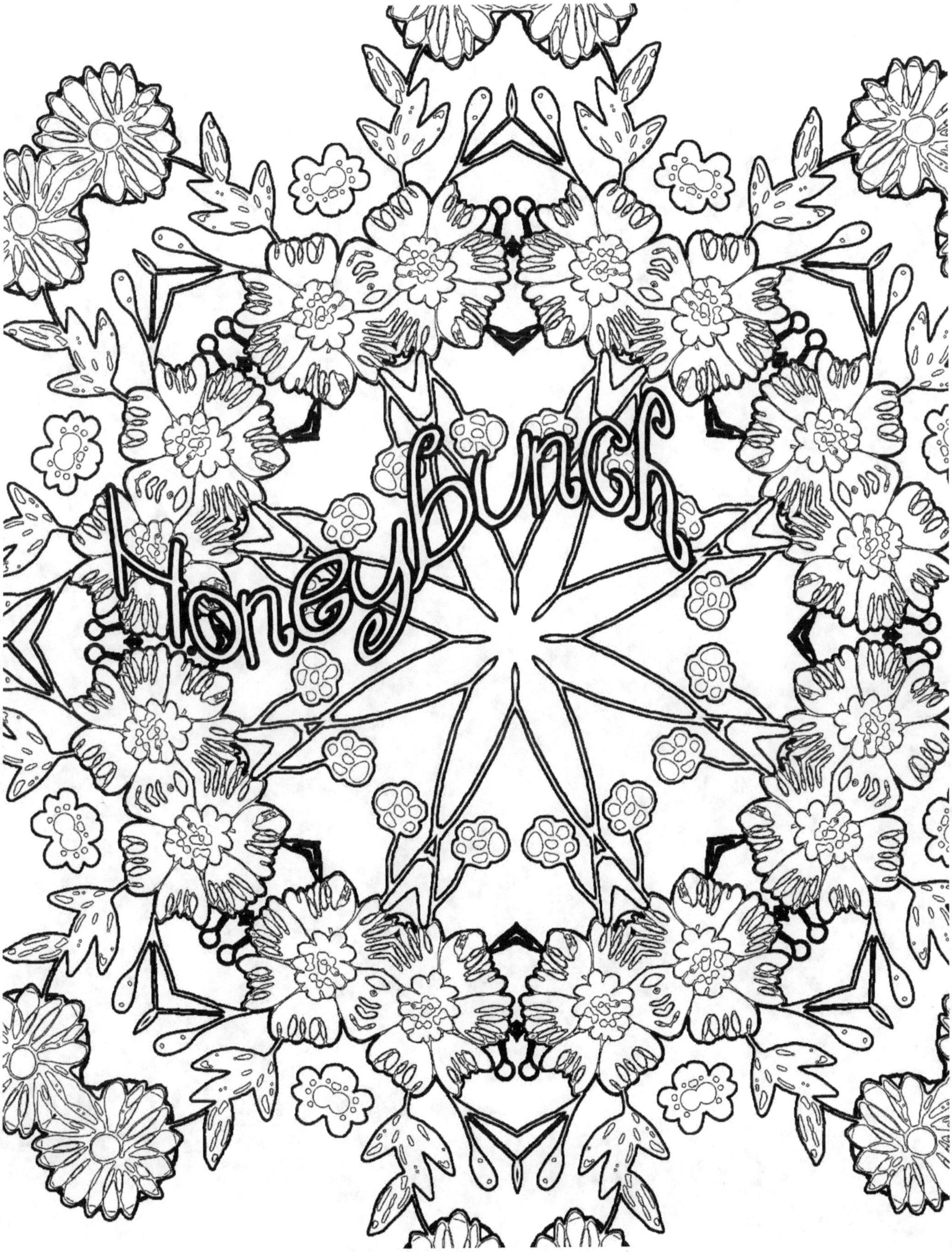
Honeybunch

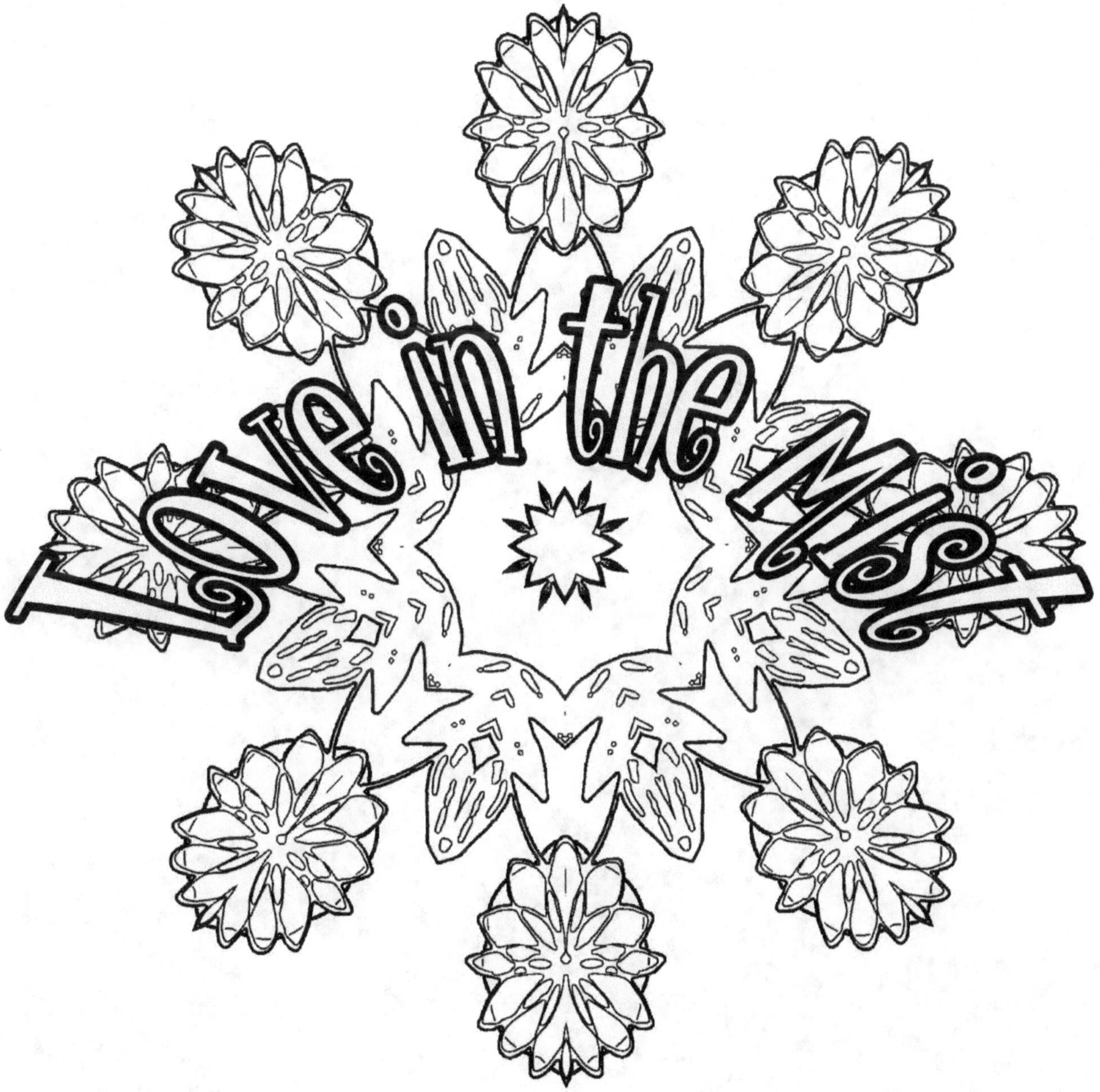
Love in the Mist

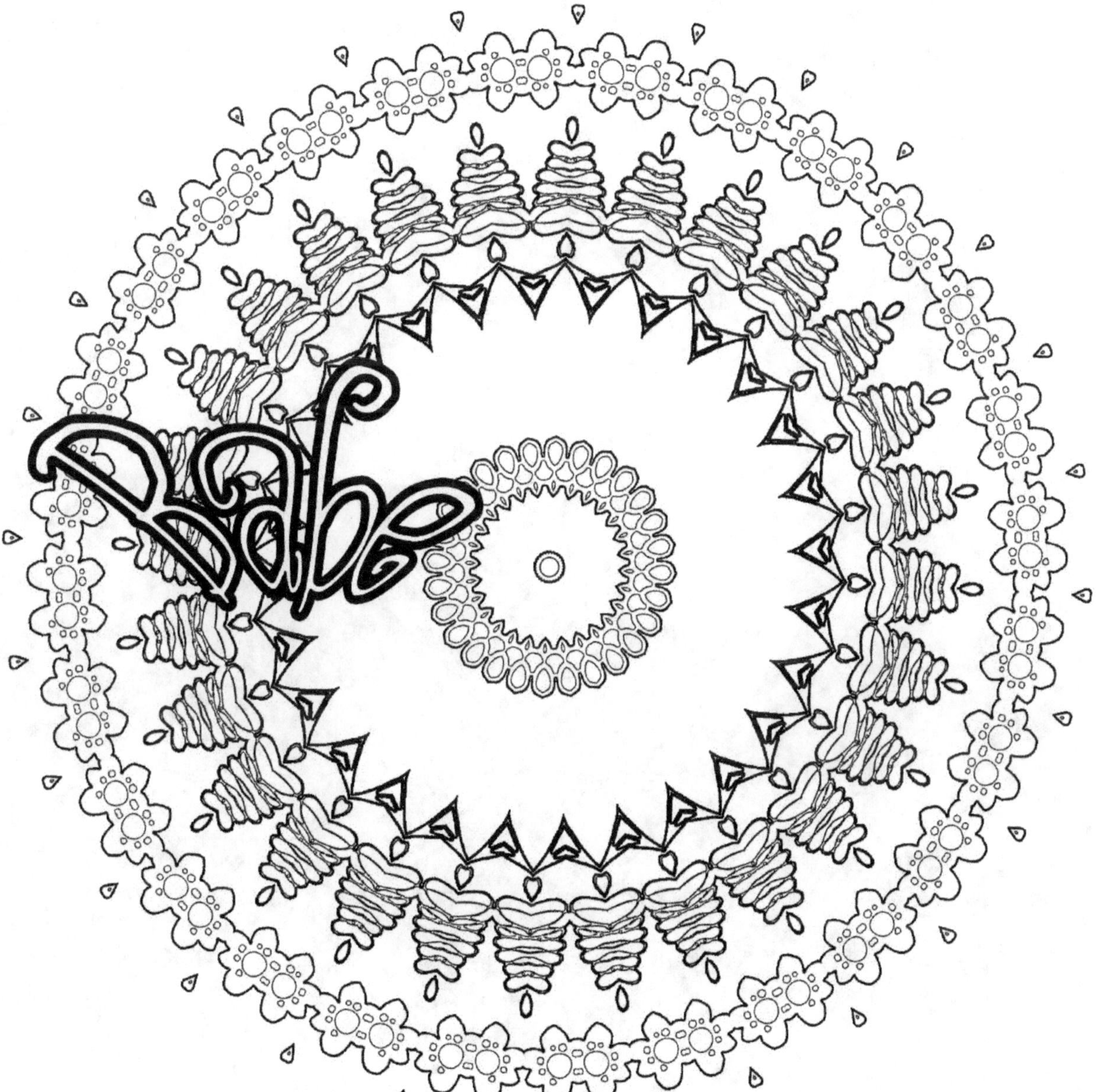
Babe

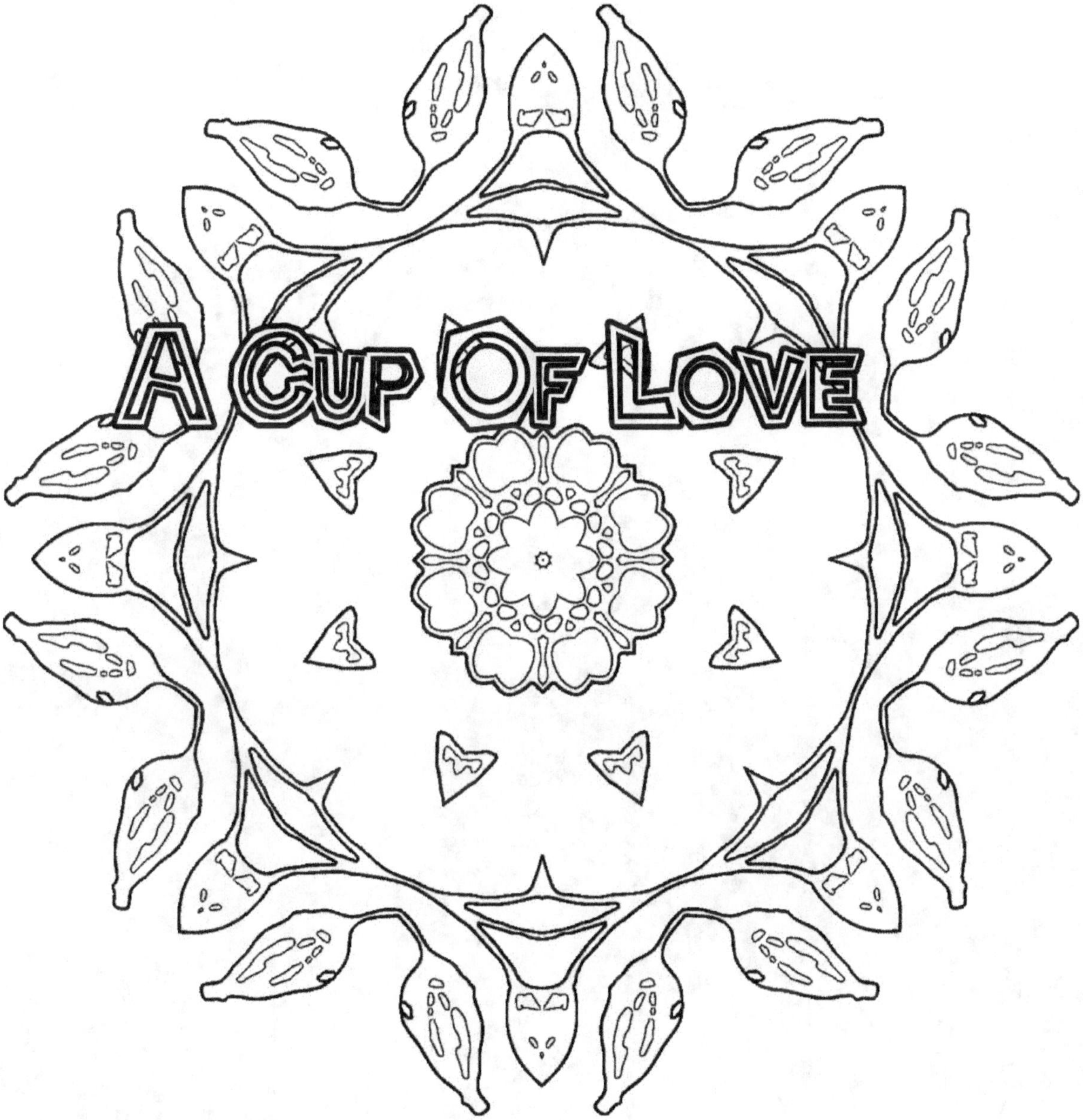
A Cup Of Love

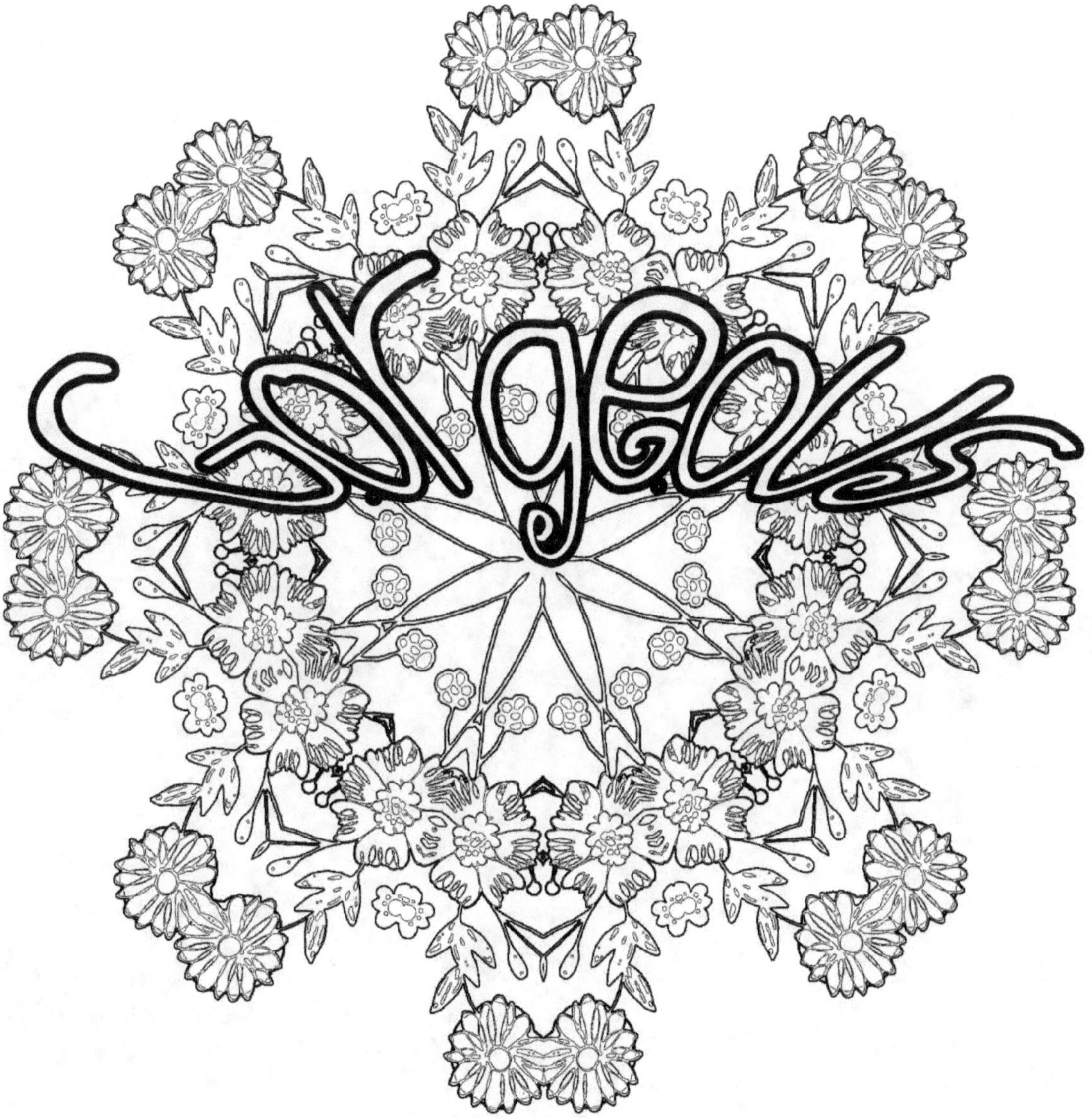
Angels

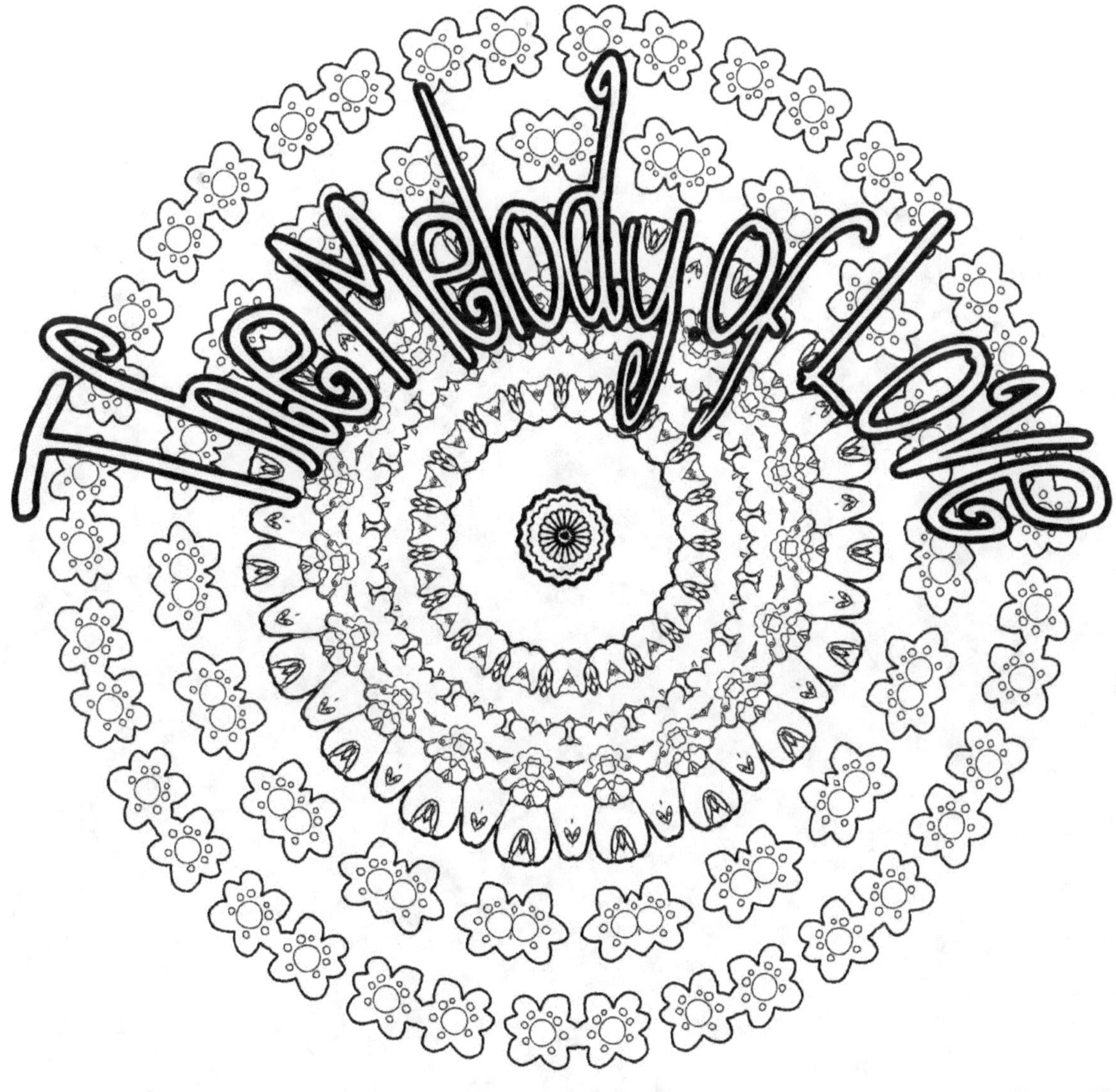
The Melody of Love

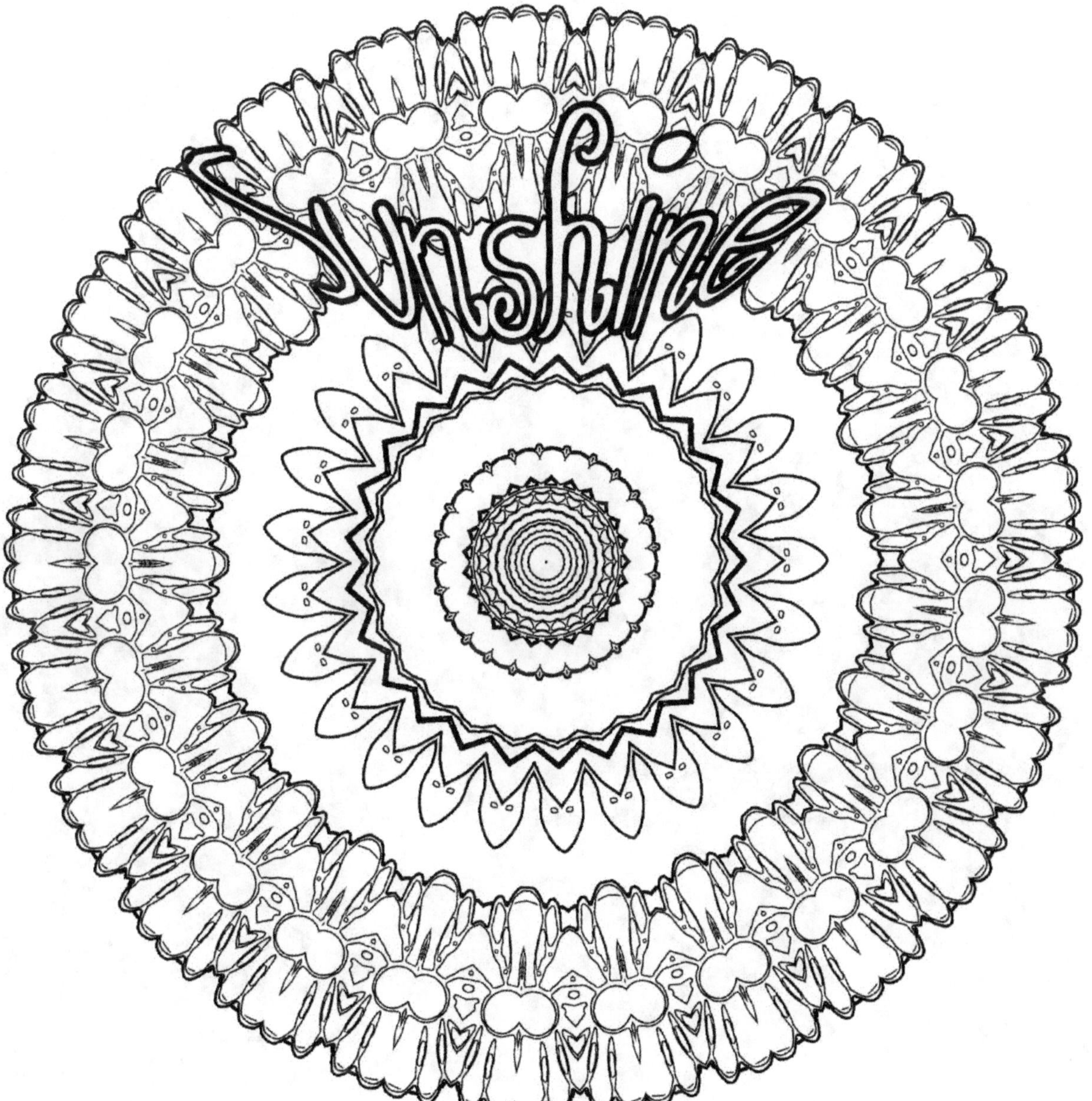
Sunshine

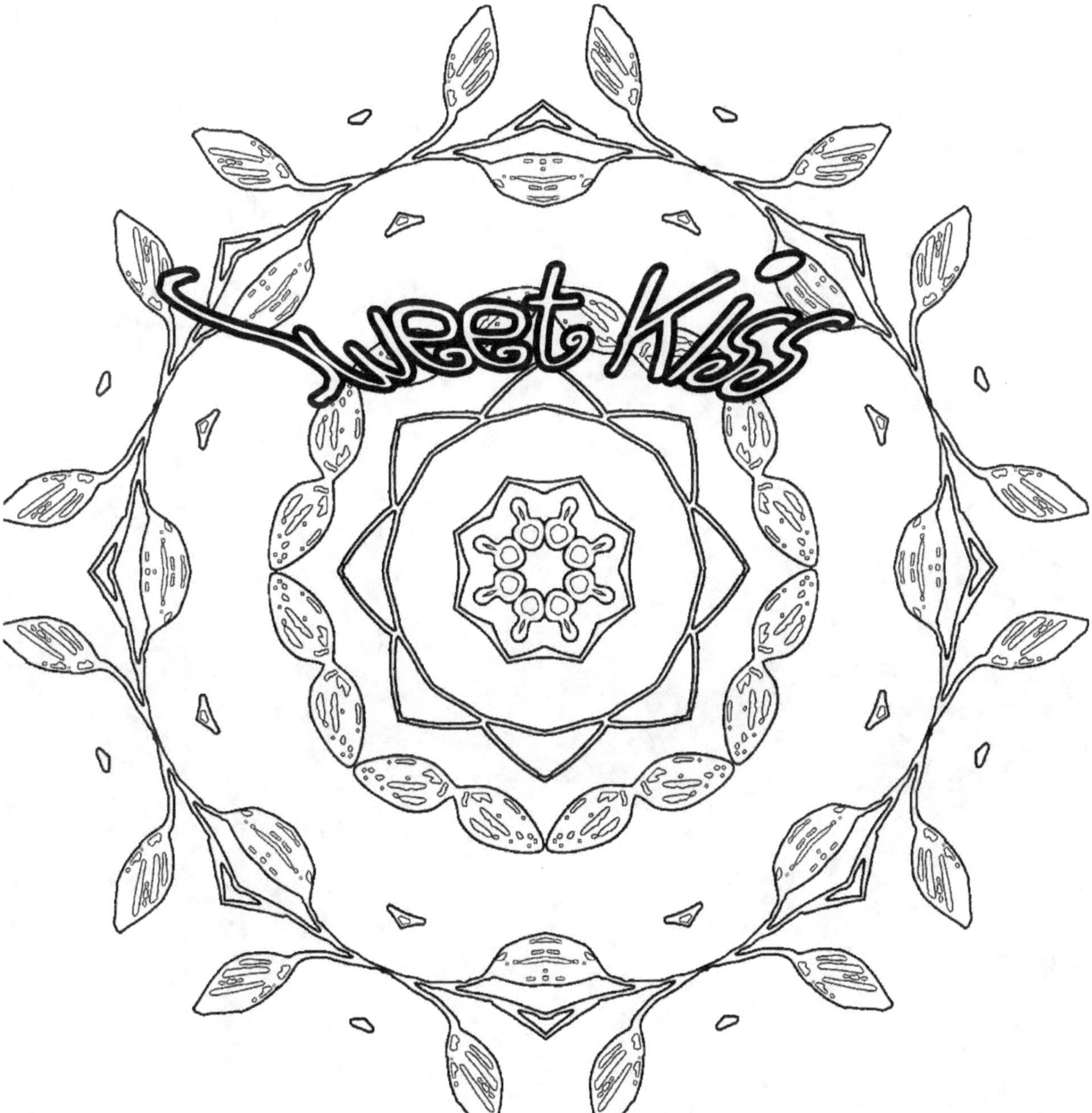
Sweet Kiss

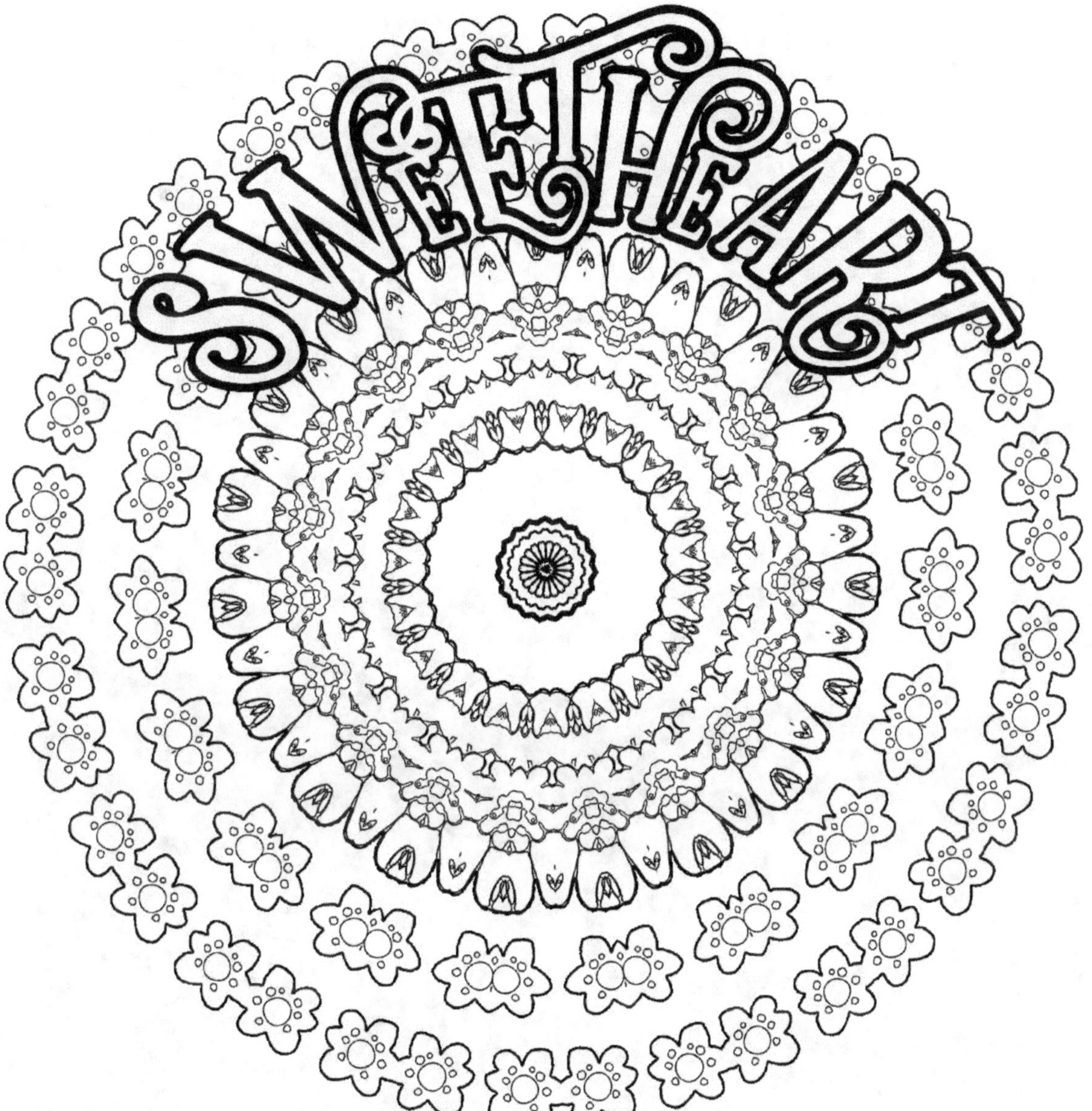
SWEETHEART

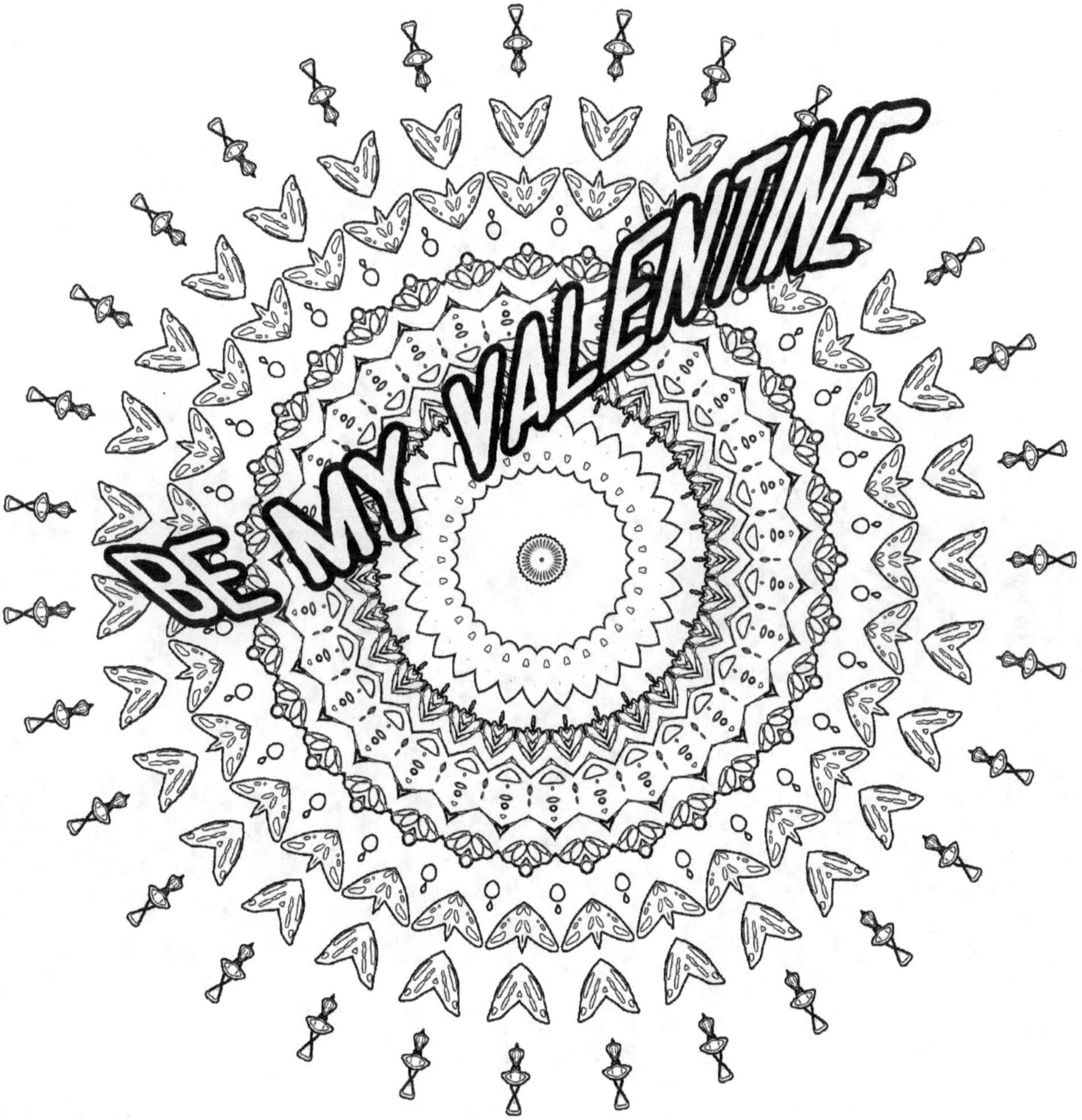
BE MY VALENTINE

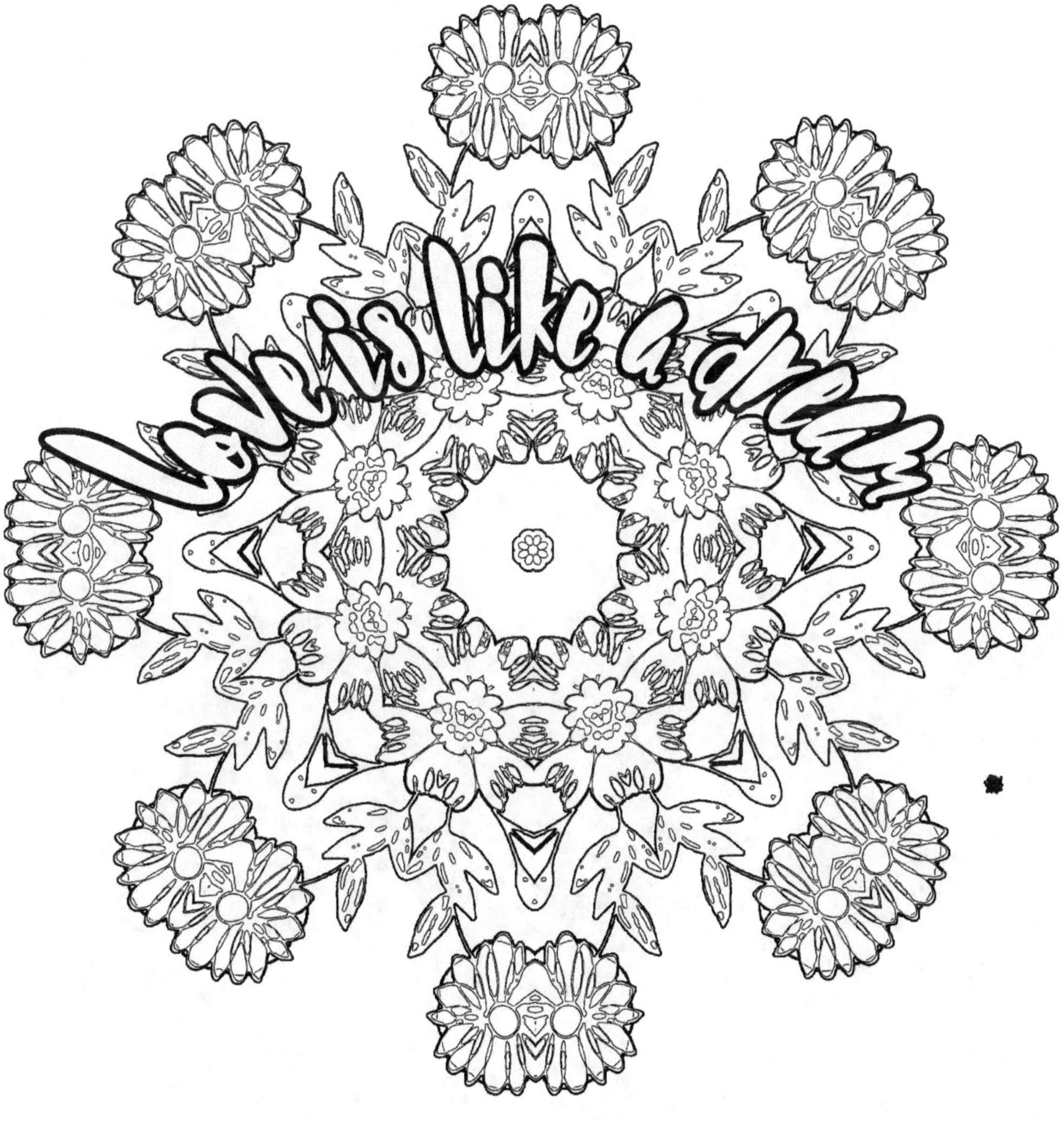
love is like a dream